D1049602

Childhood

A COMEDY IN ONE ACT

By Thornton Wilder

SAMUEL FRENCH, INC.

25 West 45th Street   NEW YORK 10036
7623 Sunset Boulevard   HOLLYWOOD 90046
LONDON   *TORONTO*

COPYRIGHT ©, 1960, BY GRANT N. NICKERSON, TRUSTEE

ALL RIGHTS RESERVED

CAUTION: Professionals and amateurs are hereby warned that CHILDHOOD is subject to a royalty. It is fully protected under the copyright laws of the United States of America, the British Empire, including the Dominion of Canada, and all other countries of the Copyright Union. All rights, including professional, amateur, motion pictures, recitation, lecturing, public reading, radio broadcasting, television and the rights of translation into foreign languages are strictly reserved. In its present form the play is dedicated to the reading public only.

CHILDREN may be given stage presentation by amateurs upon payment of a royalty of Fifteen Dollars for the first performance, and Ten Dollars for each additional performance, payable one week before the date when the play is given, to Samuel French, Inc., at 25 West 45th Street, New York, N. Y. 10036, or at 7623 Sunset Boulevard, Hollywood, Calif. 90046, or to Samuel French (Canada), Ltd., 27 Grenville Street, Toronto 5, Ontario, Canada.

Royalty of the required amount must be paid whether the play is presented for charity or gain and whether or not admission is charged.

For all other rights than those stipulated above, apply to Harold Freedman Brandt & Brandt Dramatic Dept., Inc., 101 Park Avenue, New York, N. Y. 10017.

Particular emphasis is laid on the question of amateur or professional readings, permission and terms for which must be secured in writing from Samuel French, Inc.

Copying from this book in whole or in part is strictly forbidden by law, and the right of performance is not transferable.

Whenever the play is produced the following notice must appear on all programs, printing and advertising for the play: "Produced by special arrangement with Samuel French, Inc."

Due authorship credit must be given on all programs, printing and advertising for the play.

PRINTED IN U. S. A.

CAST OF CHARACTERS
(In Order of Their Appearance)

CAROLINE

DODIE

BILLEE

MOTHER

FATHER

D37404

03740↑

Childhood

Some low chairs at the edges of the arena. These at first
represent some bushes in the yard of the children's
home. At the back, the door to the house; the aisle
through the audience serves as a path to the street.
Enter from the house CAROLINE, *twelve;* DODIE, *ten;*
and, with a rush, BILLEE, *eight.*

DODIE. Sh! Sh! Don't let Mama hear you! Car'line,
Car'line, play the game. Let's play the game.

CAROLINE. There's no time, silly. It takes time to play
the game.

BILLEE. Play Goin' to China.

CAROLINE. Don't talk so loud; we don't want Mama to
hear us. Papa'll be here soon, and we can't play the game
when Papa's here.

DODIE. Well, let's play a little. We can play Going to a
Hotel.

BILLEE. (*Clamorously.*) I want to be Room Service. I
want to be Room Service.

CAROLINE. You know Going to a Hotel takes *hours*. It's
awful when you have to stop for something.

DODIE. (*Quickly.*) Car'line, listen, I heard Mama tele-
phoning Papa and the car's got to be fixed and Papa's got
to come home by a bus, and maybe he'll never get here
and we can play for a long time.

CAROLINE. Did she say that? Well, come behind the
bushes and think.

(*They squat on their haunches behind the bushes.*)

BILLEE. Let's play Hospital and take everything out of
Dodie.

CAROLINE. Let me think a minute.

MOTHER. (*At the door.*) Caroline! Dodie! (*Silence.*) Dodie, how often do I have to tell you to hang your coat up properly? Do you know what happened? It fell and got caught under the cupboard door and was dragged back and forth. I hope it's warm Sunday, because you can't wear that coat. Billee, stand out for a moment where I can see you. Are you ready for your father when he comes home? Come out of the bushes. Billee, come out. (BILLEE, *a stoic already, comes to the Center of the Stage and stands for inspection.* MOTHER *shakes her head in silence; then:*) I simply despair. Look at you! What are you children doing anyway? Now, Caroline, you're not playing one of those games of yours? I absolutely forbid you to play that the house is on fire. You have nightmares all night long. Or those awful games about hospitals. Really, Caroline, why can't you play Shopping or Going to School? (*Silence.*) I declare. I give up. I really do. (*False exit.*) Now remember, it's Friday night, the end of the week, and you give your father a good big kiss when he comes home. (*She goes out.*)

(BILLEE *rejoins his sisters.*)

DODIE. (*Dramatic whisper.*) Car'line, let's play Funeral! (*Climax.*) Car'line, let's play ORPHANS!

CAROLINE. We haven't time—*that* takes all day. Besides, I haven't got the black gloves.

(BILLEE *sees his* FATHER *coming through the audience. Utter and final dismay.*)

BILLEE. Look't! Look!
DODIE. What?
ALL THREE. It's Papa! It's Papa!

(*They fly into the house like frightened pigeons.* FATHER *enters jauntily through the audience. It's warm, and he carries his coat over his shoulder. Arriving at the Center of the Stage, he places his coat on the ground, whistles a signal call to his wife, and swinging an imaginary golf club, executes a mighty and very successful shot.)*

FATHER. Two hundred and fifty yards!

MOTHER. (*Enters, kisses him and picks up the coat.*) Why, you're early, after all.

FATHER. Jerry drove me to the corner. Picked up a little flask for the weekend.

MOTHER. Well, I wish you wouldn't open your little flask when the children are around.

FATHER. (*Preparing a difficult shot.*) Eleventh hole. . . . Where *are* the children?

MOTHER. They were here a minute ago. They're out playing somewhere . . . Your coat on the ground! Really, you're as bad as Dodie.

FATHER. Well, you should teach the children—little trouble with the dandelions here—that it's their first duty . . . when their father comes home on Friday nights . . . (*Shouts.*) Fore, you bastards! . . . to rush toward their father . . . to grovel . . . abject thanks to him who gave them life.

MOTHER. (*Amused exasperation.*) Oh, stop that nonsense!

FATHER. On Friday nights . . . after a week of toil at the office . . . a man wants to see . . . (*He swings.*) his wives and children clinging to his knees, tears pouring down their cheeks. (*He stands up very straight, holding an enormous silver cup.*) Gentlemen, I accept this championship cup, but I wish also to give credit to my wife and children, who drove me out of the house every Sunday morning . . . Where *are* the children? Caroline! Dodie!

MOTHER. Oh, they're hiding somewhere.

FATHER. Hiding? Hiding from their father?

MOTHER. They're playing one of those awful games of

theirs. Listen to me, Fred: those games are morbid; they're dangerous.

FATHER. How do you mean, dangerous?

MOTHER. Really! No one told me when I was a bride that children are half crazy. I only hear fragments of the games, naturally, but do you realize that they like nothing better than to imagine us—away?

FATHER. Away?

MOTHER. Yes—dead?

FATHER. (*His eye on the shot.*) One . . . two . . . *three!* Well, you know what *you* said.

MOTHER. What did I say?

FATHER. *Your* dream.

MOTHER. Pshaw!

FATHER. (*Softly, with lowest insinuation.*) Your dream that . . . you and I . . . on a Mediterranean cruise . . .

MOTHER. It was Hawaii.

FATHER. And that we were—ahem!—somehow . . . *alone.*

MOTHER. Well, I didn't imagine them *dead!* I imagined them with Mother . . . or Paul . . . or their Aunt Henrietta.

FATHER. (*Piously.*) I hope so.

MOTHER. You're a brute, and everybody knows it . . . It's Caroline. She's the one who starts it all. And afterwards she has those nightmares. Come in. You'll see the children at supper.

FATHER. (*Looking upward.*) What has the weather man predicted for tomorrow?

MOTHER. (*Starting for the house.*) Floods. Torrents. You're going to stay home from the golf club and take care of the children. And I'm going to the Rocky Mountains . . . and to China.

FATHER. You'll be back by noon. What does Caroline say in her nightmares?

MOTHER. Oh! When she's awake, too. You and I are—away. Do you realize that that girl is mad about black gloves?

FATHER. Nonsense.

MOTHER. Caroline would be in constant mourning if she could manage it. Come in, come in. You'll see them at supper. (*She goes out.*)

FATHER. (*He strolls to the end of the Stage farthest from the house and calls.*) Caroline! (*Pause.*) Dodie! (*Pause.*) Bill-eeee! (*Silence. He broods aloud, his eyes on the distance.*) No instrument has yet been discovered that can read what goes on in another's mind, asleep or awake. And I hope there never will be. But once in a while, it would help a lot. Is it wrong of me to wish that . . . just once . . . I could be an invisible witness to one of my children's dreams, to one of their games? (*He calls again.*) Caroline!

(*We are in the game which is a dream. The* CHILDREN *enter as he calls them, but he does not see them and they do not see him. They come in and stand shoulder to shoulder as though they were about to sing a song before an audience.* CAROLINE *carries a child's suitcase and one of her mother's handbags; she is wearing black gloves.* DODIE *also has a suit-case and handbag, and no gloves.*)

CAROLINE. Dodie! Hurry before they see us.

FATHER. Dodie!

DODIE. Where's Billee gone?

FATHER. (*Being bumped into by* BILLEE *as he joins his sisters.*) Billee!

(FATHER *enters the house.* MOTHER *glides out of the house and takes her place at the further end of the Stage and turns and faces the* CHILDREN. *She is wearing a black hat, deep-black veil, and black gloves. Her air is one of mute acquiescent grief.* CAROLINE *glances frequently at her* MOTHER *as though for prompting. A slight formal pause.*)

CAROLINE. I guess, first, we have to say how sorry we

are. (*To* MOTHER.) Shall we begin? (MOTHER *lowers her head slightly*.) This first part is in church. Well, in a kind of church. And there's been a perfectly terrible accydent, an airplane accydent.

DODIE. (*Quickly*.) No, it was an automobile accydent.

CAROLINE. (*Ditto*.) It was an airplane.

DODIE. (*Ditto*.) I don't want it to be an airplane.

BILLEE. (*Fiercely*.) It was on a ship. It was a *big* shipwreck.

CAROLINE. Now, I'm not going to play this game unless you be quiet. It was an airplane accydent. And . . . They were on it, and they're not here any more.

BILLEE. They got *dead*.

CAROLINE. (*Glaring at him*.) Don't say that *word*. You promised you wouldn't say that word. (*Uncomfortable pause*.) And we're very sad. And . . .

DODIE. (*Brightly*.) We didn't see it, though.

CAROLINE. And we'd have put on black dresses, only we haven't got any. But we want to thank Miss Wilkerson for coming today and for wearing black like she's wearing. (MOTHER *again lowers her head*.) Miss Wilkerson is the best teacher in Benjamin Franklin School, and she's the grownup we like best.

BILLEE. (*Suddenly getting excited*.) That's not Miss Wilkerson. That's—I mean—*look!*

CAROLINE. I can't hear a word you're saying, and anyway, don't talk now!

BILLEE. (*Too young to enter the dream; pulling at his* SISTERS' *sleeves urgently*.) That's not Miss Wilkerson. That's *Mama!*

DODIE. What's the matter with your eyes?

CAROLINE. Mama's not here any more. She went away.

BILLEE. (*Staring at* MOTHER, *and beginning to doubt*.) It's . . . Mrs. Fenwick!

CAROLINE. (*Low but strongly*.) No-o-o-o! (*Resuming the ceremony*.) It wasn't so sad about Grandma, because she was more'n a hundred anyway.

DODIE. And she used to say all the time, "I won't be

with you always," and things like that, and how she'd give Mama her pearl pin.

BILLEE. I guess she's glad she isn't any more.

CAROLINE. (*Uncertainly.*) So . . .

DODIE. (*To* MOTHER, *with happy excitement.*) Are we orphans now—real orphans? (MOTHER, *always with lowered eyes, nods slightly.*) And we don't have to *do things* any more?

CAROLINE. (*Severely.*) Dodie! Don't *say* everything. (*She consults her* MOTHER.) What do I say now?

MOTHER. (*Almost inaudibly.*) About your father . . .

CAROLINE. Yes. Papa was a very fine man. And . . .

DODIE. (*Quickly.*) He used to swear bad words.

BILLEE. (*Excitedly.*) All the *time!* He'd swear swear-words.

CAROLINE. Well, maybe a little.

DODIE. He *did*. I used to want to *die*.

CAROLINE. Well, nobody's perfeck. (*Slower.*) He was all right, sometimes.

DODIE. He used to laugh too loud in front of people. And he didn't give Mama enough money to buy clothes. She had to go to town in rags, in terrible old rags.

BILLEE. (*Always excited.*) Papa'd go like this, (*Pumping his arms up and down in desperation.*) "I haven't got it! I haven't got it! You can't squeeze blood out of a stone."

DODIE. Yes, he did.

BILLEE. And Mama'd say: "I'm ashamed to go out in the street." It was awful. And then he'd say, "I'll have to mortgage, that's what I'll have to do."

CAROLINE. Billee! How can you say such an awful word? Don't you ever say that again. Papa wasn't perfeck, but he would never have done a mortgage.

BILLEE. Well, that's what he said.

CAROLINE. (*Emphatically.*) Most times Papa did his best. Everybody makes some mistakes.

DODIE. (*Demurely.*) He used to drink some, too.

BILLEE. (*Beside himself again.*) He used to drink

oceans. And Mama'd say, "Don't you think you've had enough?" and he'd say, "Down the hatch!"

DODIE. Yes, he did. And, "Just a hair of the dog that bit him." And Mama'd say, "Well, if you want to kill yourself before our eyes!" I used to want to die.

CAROLINE. Billee, don't get so excited; and you too, Dodie. Papa was a very fine man, and he *tried*. Only . . . only . . . (*Reluctantly*.) he didn't ever say anything very inneresting.

DODIE. He was inneresting when he told about the automobile accydent he'd seen and all the blood.

BILLEE. Yes, he was. But he stopped in the middle when Mama said, "Not before the children."

DODIE. Yes, he stopped then.

CAROLINE. Anyway, we're very sad. And . . . (*She looks to her* MOTHER *for prompting*.)

MOTHER. (*Almost inaudibly*.) Your mother . . .

CAROLINE. Yes. About Mama.

BILLEE. (*Hot indignation*.) Mama's almost never home. She's always shopping and having her hair made. And one time she was away *years*, to see Grandma in Boston.

DODIE. It was only five days, and Grandma was very sick.

BILLEE. No, it wasn't. It was years and years.

DODIE. Well, when she was away she didn't have to say Don't— Don't— Don't all the time, all day and night, Don't— Don't— Don't.

BILLEE. (*Tentatively defending her*.) Sometimes she makes good things to eat.

DODIE. Beans and mash potatoes, and I just hate them. "Now, you eat every mouthful, or you don't leave the table." Ugh!

CAROLINE. (*Recalling them to the ceremony*.) It wasn't her fault! Only she didn't unnerstand children. I guess there's not one in a hundred hundred that unnerstands children. (*To* MOTHER.) Is that enough, Miss Wilkerson? I can't think of anything else to say. And we've got to hurry, or Uncle Paul will come to get us, or Aunt Henrietta, or somebody even worse. So can we go now?

MOTHER. (*A whisper.*) I think it would be nice, you know, if you said how you loved them, and how they loved you.

CAROLINE. Yes—uh . . .

DODIE. It was awful when they got huggy and kissy. And when we got back an hour late, from Mary Louise's picnic, and Mama said, "I was frantic! I was frantic! I didn't know what had become of you."

CAROLINE. (*Slowly.*) She liked us best when we were sick and when I broke my arm.

DODIE. Yes. (*Exhausted pause.*) Miss Wilkerson, orphans don't have to be sad *all* the time, do they?

(MOTHER *shakes her head slightly.*)

BILLEE. Do we get any money for being orphans?

CAROLINE. We won't need it. Papa used to keep an envelope behind the clock with money in it, for accydents and times like that. I have it here. (*She goes to* MOTHER, *like a hostess getting rid of a guest.*) Thank you for coming, Miss Wilkerson. We have to go now. And thank you for wearing black.

DODIE. (*Also shaking hands; conventionally.*) Thank you very much.

(MOTHER, *with bowed head, glides into the house.*)

CAROLINE. Now be quiet, and I'll tell you what we're going to do. We've got to hurry, so don't interrupt me. We're orphans and we don't have anybody around us or near us and we're going to take a bus. (*Sensation.*) All over the world. We're going to be different persons and we're going to change our names. (*Gravely she opens her suitcase. She takes out and puts on a hat and fur neckpiece of her mother's. She looks adorable.*) I'm Mrs. Arizona. Miss Wilson, please get ready for the trip.

Dodie. Wha-a-t?

Caroline. *Miss Wilson!* Will you put your hat on, please.

Dodie. Oh! (*She puts on a hat from her suitcase.*) I want to be married, too. I want to be Mrs. Wilson.

Caroline. You're too young. People would laugh at you. We'll be gone for years and years, and by and by, in China or somewhere, you can gradually be Mrs. Wilson.

Billee. I want to be somebody, too.

Caroline. You're only *eight!* If you don't cry all the time and say awful things, I'll give you a real name. Now we can start.

Billee. But aren't Papa and Mama coming? (*The* Girls *turn and glare at him.*) Oh! they're *dead.* (*More glaring.*)

Caroline. All right. S-s-stay at home and go to s-s-school, if you want to. Papa and Mama are *happy.* Papa's playing golf and Mama's shopping. Are you ready, Miss Wilson?

Dodie. Yes, Mrs. Arizona, thank you.

Caroline. Don't run, but if we hurry we can each get a seat by the window.

(Father *enters, wearing a bus conductor's cap and big dark glasses. He casually arranges the chairs so as to indicate some of the seats of a long bus pointing toward the exit through the audience. The* Children *form a line at the door of the bus, tickets in hand.*)

Father. Take your places in line, please. The first stop, ladies and gentlemen, will be Ashagorra-Kallapalla, where there will be twenty minutes for lunch. That's the place where you get to eat the famous heaven-fruit sandwich. (*He starts punching the tickets of some imaginary passengers who precede the children.*) That cat won't be happy, madam. That's our experience. (*Severely, palping a passenger.*) You haven't got mumps, have you? Well, I'd appreciate it if you sat at a distance from the other passengers.

BILLEE. (*Staggered.*) But that's Papa!

DODIE. Don't be silly, Papa's *away*.

BILLEE. But it looks like Papa . . . and . . . (*Losing assurance.*) it looks like Dr. Summers, too.

CAROLINE. Billy, I don't know what's the matter with you. Papa wouldn't be working as a bus conductor. Papa's a man that's got more money than that.

FATHER. (*To* CAROLINE.) Your ticket, please, madam.

CAROLINE. We want to go to all the places you're going to, please.

FATHER. But you mean this to be a round-trip ticket, don't you? You're coming back, aren't you?

CAROLINE. (*None too sure; her eyes avoiding his.*) Well, maybe I won't.

FATHER. (*Lowering his voice, confidentially.*) I'll punch it on the side here. That'll mean you can use it, whenever you want, to come back here. (CAROLINE *takes her place on the bus.* MOTHER *glides in and takes her place in the line behind* BILLEE. *She is now wearing a brown hat and a deep-brown veil.* FATHER *punches* DODIE'S *ticket.*) Why, I think I've seen your face before, madam. Weren't you in that terrible automobile accident—blood all over the road and everything?

DODIE. (*Embarrassed; low.*) No, no, I wasn't.

FATHER. Well, I'm glad to hear that. (DODIE *takes her seat behind* CAROLINE. *To* BILLEE, *punching his ticket.*) And what's your name, sir, if I may ask?

BILLEE. Billee.

CAROLINE. (*Officiously.*) His name is Mr. Wentworth.

FATHER. Mr. Wentworth. Good morning. (*Man to man, with a touch of severity.*) No smoking in the first six rows, watch that, and . . . (*Significant whisper.*) there'll be no liquor drinking on this bus. I hope that's understood. (BILLEE, *considerably intimidated, takes his place behind* DODIE. *During the following he sees* MOTHER *and stares at her in amazement.* FATHER *punches* MOTHER'S *ticket, saying in sad condolence:*) I hope you have a good trip, ma'am. I hope you have a good trip.

MOTHER. (*A whisper.*) Thank you. (*She takes a place in the last row.*)

CAROLINE. (*Rummaging in her handbag.*) Would you like a candy bar, Miss Wilson . . . and Mr. Wentworth?

DODIE. Thank you, Mrs. Arizona, I would.

BILLEE. Look! LOOK! That's Mama!

DODIE. Stop poking me. It's not. It's *not*.

FATHER. Well, now, all aboard that's going to go. (*He climbs on the bus, takes his seat, tries his gears, then rises and addresses the passengers weightily.*) Before we start, there are some things I want to say about this trip. *Bus travel is not easy.* I think you'll know what I mean, Mrs. Arizona, when I say that it's like family life: we're all stuck in this vehicle together. We go through some pretty dangerous country, and I want you all to keep your heads. Like when we go through the Black Snake Indian territory, for instance. I've just heard they're getting a little —restless. And along the Kappikappi River, where all those lions and tigers are, and other things. Now, I'm a pretty good driver, but nobody's perfect and everybody can make a mistake once in a while. But I don't want any complaints afterward that you weren't warned. If anybody wants to get off this bus and go home, this is the moment to do it, and I'll give you your money back. (*Indicating* MOTHER.) There's one passenger here I know can be counted on. She's made the trip before and she's a regular crackerjack. Excuse me praising you to your face, ma'am, but I mean every word of it. Now, how many of you have been trained in first aid—will you hold up your hands? (BILLEE *and* MOTHER *raise their hands promptly.* CAROLINE *and* DODIE *look at one another uncertainly but do not raise their hands.*) Well, we may have to hold some classes later—go to school, so to speak. Accidents are always likely to happen when we get to the tops of the mountains. So! I guess we're ready to start. When we start, we often have a word of prayer if there's a minister of the gospel on board. (*To* BILLEE.) May I ask if you're a minister of the gospel, Mr. Wentworth?

BILLEE. N-no.

FATHER. Then we'll just have to *think* it. (*Lowering his voice, to* BILLEE.) And, may I add, I hope that there won't be any bad language used on this bus. There are ladies present—and some very fine ladies, too, if I may say so. Well, here we go! Forward march.

CAROLINE. (*To* DODIE, *confidentially*.) If it's going to be so dangerous, I think we'd better move up a little nearer *him*.

(*They slip across the aisle and slide, side by side, into the second row behind* FATHER. BILLEE *has gone to the back of the car and stands staring at* MOTHER.)

BILLEE. (*Indicating the veil*.) Do you ever take that off?

MOTHER. (*Softly, lowered eyes*.) Sometimes I do.

CAROLINE. Billee! Don't disturb the lady. Come and sit by us.

MOTHER. Oh, he's not disturbing me at all.

(*Soon he takes the seat beside her, and she puts her arm around him*.)

FATHER. (*As he drives, talking to the* GIRLS *over his shoulder*.) It's hard work driving a bus, ladies. Did you ever think of that?

CAROLINE. Oh, yes. It must be hard.

FATHER. Sometimes I wonder why I do it. Mornings . . . leave my house and family and get on the bus. And it's no fun, believe me. (*Jerk*.) See that? Almost ran over that soldier. And—would you believe it—I don't get much money for it.

CAROLINE. (*Breathless interest*.) Don't they pay you a *lot*?

FATHER. Mrs. Arizona, I'm telling you the truth: sometimes I wonder if we're going to have enough to eat.

DODIE. Why, I think that's terrible!

FATHER. And if I can get enough clothes to wear. I see that's a nice furpiece you have on, Mrs. Arizona.

CAROLINE. Oh, this is *old*.

DODIE. (*Very earnestly.*) But at your house you do have breakfast and lunch and supper, don't you?

FATHER. Miss Wilson, you're awfully kind to ask. So far we have. Sometimes it's just, you know, beans and things like that. Life's not easy, Mrs. Arizona. You must have noticed that.

BILLEE. (*Big alarm.*) Mr. Bus Conductor, look't. Look over there!

FATHER. (*Galvanized;* ALL *stare toward the Left.*) Ladies and gentlemen, there are those goldarn Indians again! I want you to put your heads right down on the floor! Right down! (ALL *except* FATHER *crouch on the floor.*) I don't want any of them arrows to come in the windows and hit you. (FATHER *fires masterfully from the hip.*) They'll be sorry for this. BANG! BANG! That'll teach them. BANG! (BILLEE *rises and whirls, shooting splendidly in all directions.*) There! The danger's over, ladies and gentlemen. You can get in your seats now. I'll report that to the Man Up There in Washington, D.C., you see if I don't. (*To* MOTHER.) May I ask if you're all right back there?

MOTHER. Yes, thank you, Mr. Bus Conductor. I want to say that Mr. Wentworth behaved splendidly. I don't think that I'd be here except for him.

FATHER. Good! Minute I saw him I knew he had the old stuff in him! Ladies, I think you did A-number-one, too.

CAROLINE. Does that happen often, Mr. Bus Conductor?

FATHER. Well, you know what a man's life is like, Mrs. Arizona. Fight. Struggle. Survive. Struggle. Survive. Always was.

DODIE. What if—what if you *didn't* come back?

FATHER. Do you mean, if I died? We don't think of that, Miss Wilson. But when we come home Friday nights we like to see the look on the faces of our wives and children. Another week, and we're still there. And do you know what I do on my free days, Miss Wilson, after sitting cooped up behind this wheel?

DODIE. (*Sudden inspiration.*) Play golf.

FATHER. You're bright, Miss Wilson, bright as a penny.

CAROLINE. (*Who has been glancing at* MOTHER.) Mr. Bus Conductor, can I ask you why that lady—why she's so sad?

FATHER. You don't know?

CAROLINE. No.

FATHER. (*Lowering his voice.*) She just got some bad news. Her children left the house.

CAROLINE. Did they?

FATHER. Don't mention it to her, will you?

CAROLINE. (*Insecurely.*) Why did they do that?

FATHER. Well, children are funny. Funny. Now I come to think of it, it'd be nice if, a little later, you went back and sort of comforted her. Like Mr. Wentworth's doing.

DODIE. Wasn't she good to them?

FATHER. What's that?

DODIE. Wasn't she a *good* mother?

FATHER. Well, let me ask *you* a question: is there any such thing as a good mother or a good father? Look at me: I do the best I can for my family—things to eat, you know, and dresses and shoes. I see you've got some real pretty shoes on, ladies. But, well, *children don't understand,* and that's all you can say about it. Do you know what one of my daughters said to me last week? She said she wished she was an orphan. Hard. Very hard.

CAROLINE. (*Struggling.*) Lots of times parents don't understand children, either.

FATHER. (*Abruptly breaking the mood.*) But now, ladies and gentlemen, I have a treat for you. (*Stops the bus and points dramatically to the front Right.* ALL *gaze in awe.*) Isn't that a sight! The Mississippi River! Isn't that a lot of water!

MOTHER. (*After a moment's gaze, with increasing concern.*) But—but—Mr. Bus Conductor.

FATHER. (*Looking back at her and sharing her anxiety.*) Madam, I think I know what you're thinking, and it troubles me too. (MOTHER *has come halfway down the aisle, her eyes on the river.*) Ladies and gentlemen, the river's in flood. I don't think I've ever seen it so high. The question is: would it be safe to cross it today? Look yourselves—would that bridge hold?

MOTHER. (*Returning to her seat.*) Mr. Bus Conductor, may I make a suggestion?

FATHER. You certainly may.

MOTHER. I suggest that you ask the passengers to raise their hands if they think it's best that we don't cross the Mississippi today.

FATHER. *Very* good idea! That'll mean we turn around and go back to where we came from. Now think it over, ladies and gentlemen. All who are ready to do that raise their hands. (MOTHER *and* BILLEE *raise their hands at once. Then* DODIE. *Finally, unhappily,* CAROLINE. FATHER *earnestly counts the twenty hands in the bus.*) All right! Everybody wants to go back. So, here we go. (*He starts the bus.*) Now, I'm going to go pretty fast, so sit square in your seats. (*After a pause, confidentially over his shoulder to* CAROLINE.) I hope you really meant it when you put your hand up, Mrs. Arizona.

CAROLINE. Well . . .

FATHER. You *do* have some folks waiting for you at home, don't you?

DODIE. (*Quickly.*) Yes, we do.

CAROLINE. (*Slowly, near to tears.*) But we didn't get to China or to that river where the lions and tigers are. It's too soon to go back to where I come from, where everybody says silly things they don't mean one bit, and where nobody treats you like a real person. And we didn't get to eat the famous heaven-fruit sandwich at that place.

DODIE. (*Embarrassed.*) Car'line, you can do it another time.

(CAROLINE'S *lowered head shows that she doesn't believe this.*)

FATHER. (*Confidentially.*) Mrs. Arizona, I'll honor that ticket *at any time*, and I'll be looking for you.

CAROLINE. (*Raises her eyes to him gravely; after a minute she says, also in a low voice.*) Mr. Bus Conductor—

FATHER. Yes, Mrs. Arizona.

CAROLINE. Do you get paid just the same, even if you didn't go the whole way?

FATHER. I? Oh, don't you think of that, ma'am. We can tighten our belts. There's always something.

CAROLINE. (*Groping feverishly in her handbag, with a quick sob.*) No! I haven't got a *lot* of money, but—here! Here's more'n two dollars, and you can buy a lot of things to eat with that.

FATHER. (*Quietly and slowly, his eyes on the road.*) That's real thoughtful of you, Mrs. Arizona, and I thank you. But you put that away and keep it. I feel sure that this is going to be my good year. (*After a pause.*) Excuse me, may I put my hand on your hand a minute to show you know I appreciate what you did?

CAROLINE. (*Shy.*) Yes, you may.

(*He does so, very respectfully; then returns to his wheel.*)

DODIE. Car'line, what're you crying about?

CAROLINE. When . . . you try to *do* something for somebody . . . and . . .

FATHER. (*Very cheerful and loud.*) Gee whillikers! My wife will be surprised to see me back home so soon. Poor old thing, she doesn't have many pleasures. Just a little shopping now and then. (*He tosses off a snatch of song.*) "The son of a, son of a, son of a gambolier . . ." I think this would be a good time to go back and say a nice word to that lady who's had a little disappointment in her home, don't you?

CAROLINE. Well, uh . . . Come, Dodie. (CAROLINE *goes back and sits in front of* MOTHER, *talking to her over the back of the seat;* DODIE *stands beside her.*) The bus conductor says that everybody isn't in your house any more.

MOTHER. (*Lowered eyes.*) Did he? That's true.

CAROLINE. They'll come back. I know they will.

MOTHER. Oh, do you think so?

CAROLINE. Children don't like being treated as children *all the time.* And I think it isn't worth while being born into the world if you have to do the same things every day.

DODIE. The reason I don't like grownups is that they don't ever think any inneresting thoughts. I guess they're so old that they just get tired of expecting anything to be different or exciting. So they just do the same old golfing and shopping.

CAROLINE. (*Suddenly seeing a landmark through the window.*) Mr. Bus Conductor! Mr. Bus Conductor! Please, will you please stop at the next corner? This is where we have to get off. (*Under her voice, commandingly.*) Come, Dodie, Billee. Come quick!

(*They start up the aisle toward the bus exit, then turn back to* MOTHER. *Their farewells are their best party manners.*)

THE CHILDREN. (*Shaking hands with both* PARENTS.) I'm very glad to have met you. Thank you very much. I'm very glad to have met you.

FATHER. (*As* MOTHER *joins him at the bus exit.*) But you'll come on my bus again? We'll see you again?

CAROLINE. (*To* DODIE *and* BILLEE, *low.*) Now, run! (*They run into the house like rabbits. She stands at the bus door, with lowered eyes.*) Well . . . you see . . . you're just people in our game. You're not *really* alive. That's why we could talk to you. (*A quick glance at her* FATHER, *then she looks down again.*) Besides, we've found

that it's best not to make friends with grownups, because
. . . in the end . . . they don't act fair to you . . . But
thank you; I'm very glad to have met you.

(*She goes into the house.* FATHER *takes off his cap and
glasses;* MOTHER *her hat and veil. They place them
on chairs.* FATHER *prepares to make a difficult golf
stroke.*)

FATHER. Where *are* the children?

MOTHER. Oh, they're hiding somewhere, as usual.

FATHER. Hiding! Hiding from their father!

MOTHER. Or they're playing one of those awful games
of theirs. Come in, come in. You'll see them at supper.
(*She goes into the house.*)

FATHER. (*He stands at the end of the Stage farthest
from the house and calls.*) Caroline! Dodie! Billee-ee-ee!
(*Silence, of course. He goes into the house.*)

CURTAIN

THE RED KEY

Drama. 1 act. By Charles Emery.

1 male, 2 females. Interior. Modern costumes. 35 minutes.

Karen has come to stay with Nicholas and his mental-case sister, Hester. Nicholas and Karen's father were partners until Karen's father suddenly vanished. In a confidential mood, Hester tells Karen that the door in the room concealed by a drape has not been opened for seven years, and that a key on a red ribbon in Nicholas's possession opens the door. Remembering that it was seven years ago that her father disappeared, Karen's suspicion increases with intensity as the play gathers momentum and the red key becomes a symbol of fear and mistrust.
(Royalty, $5.00.)

FIVE FOR BAD LUCK

Comedy. 1 act. By Wm. G. B. Carson.

4 males, 4 females. Interior. Modern costumes. 30 minutes.

A class dance is about to be given in a co-educational college, and the boys have collected five dollars to be given as compensation to the "unlucky" one who draws Effie Trask. Her name has been drawn by one of the most prominent boys on the campus, a thoroughly spoiled social light. Effie learns what has happened and decides to make her hireling escort earn his five dollars. The way in which she does so is the subject of the play.
(Royalty, $5.00.)

GEORGIE—PORGIE

Comedy. 1 act. By James Reach.

3 males, 5 females. Modern costumes. 30 minutes.

It is New Year's Eve at the Spinnits'. The children are going to the hotel dance—all four of them, except fourteen-year-old Georgie. Older sister Dorothea has a quarrel with her boyfriend and sets out to steal Millie's beau. But Georgie has an ingenious plan which works, and Dorothea is foiled. Then Georgie hands older brother Tod his come-uppance, and in the end goes off to the dance in Tod's dress suit and with a brand-new girl!
(Royalty, $5.00.)

THE STOLEN PRINCE

Adventure. 1 act. By Dan Totheroh.

10 characters, extras. Setting: curtain and Chinese screens.
30 minutes.

At times comic, and at other times sad, this story is about a
prince who was stolen at birth and rescued by a poor man and
his wife. Because they inadvertently offended the emperor,
the man and wife are sentenced to die. But recognition of the
young prince saved the day for one and all and brings the
kingdom an heir. The Chinese property man makes staging
not only humorous but easy as well.

(Royalty, $5.00.)

THE LOST PRINCESS

Adventure. 1 act. By Dan Totheroh.

12 characters, extras. Setting: curtain and Chinese screens.
30 minutes.

The sequel to "The Stolen Prince" centers on the twin
sister of the prince, who was stolen away by a nurse at birth
and who grew up as the foster daughter of a mountain robber.
She reforms the robber and saves his life when she is recognized
as the princess in the end. The same quaint, comic staging will
endear this play to every audience.

(Royalty, $5.00.)

THE EMPEROR'S NIGHTINGALE

Comedy. 1 act. By Dan Totheroh.

12 characters. Setting: Chinese reversible screens. 30 minutes.

Dramatized from the story of Hans Christian Andersen. The
emperor thought that the nightingale had the sweetest song in
the world; but the nightingale felt sad locked in a cage. A lovely
mechanical nightingale was presented to the emperor, and he
turned all his attention to it. But one day it broke down, and
the emperor began to die. It remained for the real nightingale
to return and revive the emperor with its glorious song.

(Royalty, $5.00.)

ONE-ACT MUSICALS

CHAIN OF JADE

A musical version of Dan Totheroh's charming fantasy, "The Stolen Prince."

David Rogers and Mark Bucci.

8 males, 3 females. Chinese costumes. 5 songs. 35 minutes.

Wittily written in the style of the classic Chinese Theatre with a 1 man chorus who speaks directly to the audience, an indolent property man who is obliged to impersonate a duck and an onstage orchestra clanging cymbals and beating on drums.

Libretto and piano score $1.50. (Royalty, $15-$10.)

A PINK PARTY DRESS

David Rogers and Mark Bucci.

A musical version of Margaret Bland's "Pink and Patches."

1 male, 3 females. Exterior. Modern costume. 5 songs. 35 minutes.

The story of Texie, a mountain girl who hopes to escape the life of hardship and poverty her mother and other mountain women lead. She longs for the richer life she has observed at a fashionable hotel nearby and for a pink party dress instead of the patched brown denim she is forced to wear.

Libretto and piano score $1.50. (Royalty, $15-$10.)

THE OLD LADY SHOWS HER MEDALS

David Rogers and Mark Bucci.

A musical version of J. M. Barrie's "The Old Lady Shows Her Medals."

2 male, 4 female. Interior. 6 songs. 60 minutes.

Set in London during World War I. An old charlady, who is alone in the world, pretends to her friends that she, too, has a man away at the war, a son in the Black Watch Regiment.

Libretto and piano score $2.00. (Royalty, $20-$15.)

HE CAME SEEING

Biblical drama. 1 act. By Mary P. Hamlin.

3 males, 2 females. Interior. Biblical costumes.

This little Biblical play, written by the author of *The Rock*, is a dramatic presentation of the story of a young man who comes under the personal influence of Christ and casts off his earlier belief in order to embrace Christianity.

yalty, $5.00.)

I LAY IN ZION

Drama in verse. 1 act. By William Gibson.

4 males, 4 females. Interior. Costumes,
Palestinian and Roman. 40 minutes.

The high priest's palace following the arrest of Jesus. Peter comes to learn of his Master's fate. An old woman repeats to him Jesus's prediction that Peter will deny him thrice before the cock crows. Peter's wife spies in the courtroom, and reports that Jesus will be crucified. He is recognized, denies Jesus thrice, and the cock crows. Left alone, he condemns himself and all men at their worst: the old woman reminds him that this is the rock the church must be built on. Faced with a choice between safety or crucifixion in going to Rome, Peter chooses Rome and the cross.

(Royalty, $5.00.)

WHOSOEVER BELIEVETH

Biblical play. 1 act. By Lloyd Corrigan.

3 males. Interior.

The scene is Jerusalem, in the year of our Lord 33. It is a spring evening. Nathan, assisted by a maimed youth, is cleaning up after the Passover Feast which has just been celebrated by Christ and His apostles. The youth's father, who hates the Nazarene, has heard of the affair and comes to command his son home. In the ensuing dispute he discloses the coming betrayal. The youth's brilliant faith and miraculous gesture astonish the father, and he confesses the place of the betrayal. The youth runs off to warn Christ; but we know that he is already too late.

yalty, $5.00.)

IF MEN PLAYED CARDS AS WOMEN DO

by GEORGE S. KAUFMAN

Satirical comedy—1 Act

4 Men—Modern Costumes

A brilliant satire for men. The fun of this comic sketch is derived from the fact that a group of men at the bridge table speak, behave, and think after the manner in which women are supposed to conduct their game.

(Royalty, $5.00.)

THE STILL ALARM

by GEORGE S. KAUFMAN

Satirical comedy—1 Act

5 Men—Modern and Fireman's Costumes

The scene is in the bedroom of a hotel which is on fire The fun lies in the manner in which it is put out. In the face of most exciting danger, the characters play in the well-bred manner of English drawing-room actors.

(Royalty, $5.00.)

WHEN MEN REDUCE AS WOMEN DO

by OTTO KICKS

Comedy—1 Act

5 Men—Modern Costumes

What happens when a bunch of men gather and talk like women about their efforts to lose weight results in a riot of laughter.

(Royalty, $5.00.)

Early Frost

by DOUGLAS PARKHIRST

Drama—1 Act
5 Female—Interior

A tender, yet gripping story of two sisters, Hannah and Louise, who live in a rambling, old house. Hannah has been considered peculiar ever since childhood, when a missing playmate was believed carried off by gypsies. When Alice, the sisters' little niece, comes to live with them, Hannah fearfully insists that she is the missing child returned. While playing in the attic, Alice is visited by a strange illusion, which almost leads her to solve the mystery of fifty years ago. Hannah, fearing her long-guarded secret will be discovered, tries to silence the little girl. It is this tense, cat-and-mouse game between the two that brings the play to a startling climax and affords the actors an opportunity for skillful playing, while holding the audience spellbound.

(Royalty, $5.00.)

An Overpraised Season

by RICHARD S. DUNLOP

A Play of Ideas—1 Act
4 male, 2 female—No setting required

A powerful and touching story, "An Overpraised Season" won six out of nine possible awards at the one-act contest in which it premiered. Numerous problems facing today's intelligent and sensitive adolescents are treated in the 40 minute play, which, in episode form, concerns two boys and a girl; a domineering, religiously fanatic mother; and a selfish, egocentric father. A narrator, somewhat like the Stage Manager of "Our Town," expounds the philosophy of the play. A quality play, "Season" is designed for advanced student performers.

(Royalty, $5.00.)

THE INCOME TAX

Comedy. 1 act. By Peg Lynch.

3 males, 2 females. Interior. 30-40 minutes.

Anyone who has even felt the hot breath of the income tax inspector will know how Ethel and Albert feel when they get a notice that the Government wants to check their last year's tax return. Wondering if they have put down too much for charity and business expense, they await his arrival with visions of Leavenworth dancing in their heads.

(Royalty, $10.00.)

GROW UP

Morality play. 1 act. By Peggy Lamson.

3 males, 2 females. Int., ext. drop.

Tells of the problems a teen-age boy faces as he begins to emerge into the adult world. He is lackadaisical, disoriented, and sloppy; and his marks are failing. It remains for his younger brother to show the way to a proper attitude toward life.

(Royalty, $10.00.)

THE DUELLING OAKES

Comedy. 1 act. By Bruce Kimes.

2 males, 3 females. Interior.

Concerns a preposterous and manifestly outrageous duel to be fought by the newly-weds, Bill and Sally Oakes, in the living room of their home. A childish but nevertheless serious argument is started and it snowballs into a tempestuous challenge—a challenge to a duel with pistols at ten paces. The duel and its consequent results we think will delight and amuse you.

(Royalty, $5.00.)

🐝🐝🐝🐝🐝🐝🐝🐝🐝🐝🐝🐝🐝🐝🐝🐝🐝🐝🐝🐝🐝🐝🐝🐝🐝🐝

OF POEMS . . . YOUTH, and SPRING

COMEDY, 1 ACT—by JOHN LOGAN

1 male, 1 female, 3 voices; 4 chorus members

Concerns the first romance of a boy and a girl in high school. The play's four scenes correspond to the seasons of the year; and each season represents a stage in the couple's romance, spring being when they meet and winter when they part. Each season is introduced by two small choruses which, in a mood of light humor and fantasy, tease and scold and provide contrast to the light drama of the romance. They also act incidental roles in the story and perform stagehand duties.

(Royalty, $5.00.)

BRIDGES . . . Are When You Cross Them

COMEDY, 1 ACT—by MELVIN B. SHAFFER

3 male, 2 female—Interior

This American family is in San Francisco on another leg of a sightseeing tour. Father has everything laid out exactly and punctually, so that the city can be covered in one day. He does his sightseeing by telescope from the hotel window, but each of the other members of the family is given assignments and required to render reports that may be shared with the others. It's all very orderly and by-the-numbers. Except that the daughter is wayward. She's the kind who, on seeing the ocean, stays all day to enjoy it. She even begins to see things that aren't there, like the Golden Gate Bridge. The unimaginative members of the family, however, cannot see it, and so flatly state that it does not exist.

(Royalty, $5.00.)

COLUMBINE CUM LAUDE

COMEDY, 1 ACT—by LYDA NAGEL

3 males, 3 females—Interior

One fine morning Columbine awakes to find a thought in her head. This leads the pretty flirt. who has been pursuing Harlequin for five hundred years. into the arms of a stodgy professor, who whisks her away for a "mortarboard" marriage. Harlequin, always so concerned with himself. is rocked out of his boredom by the discovery that he has a broken heart. With the aid of his friend. Pierrot. Harlequin recaptures for a fleeting instant what he loves. but has he truly learned that. when we change what we most desire. we destroy it? Only Columbine knows the answer, and she will never tell.

(Royalty, $5.00.)

🐝🐝🐝🐝🐝🐝🐝🐝🐝🐝🐝🐝🐝🐝🐝🐝🐝🐝🐝🐝🐝🐝🐝🐝🐝🐝

A

812   Wilder, Thornton Niven, 1897-
          Childhood, a comedy in one act.
       New York, French [1960]
          23p.

D37404 ✓

87914

          3 1978 00096 7265

                              9-17-98

       I. Title.

                    pt
                    tes th

                                        to be a

**INDIANAPOLIS-MARION COUNTY
PUBLIC LIBRARY**

OFFERS YOU:

BOOKS   PAMPHLETS   and
RECORDS   PICTURES   ould
FILMS   PROGRAMS   been
MAGAZINES   FOR   rong
MUSIC   ADULTS   Mr.
MAPS   AND   h a
AND,   CHILDREN   ing.
                                  ows
                                   an
                                  bits
                                  ocks
                                  and
                                   us

[OTHER BORROWERS WILL APPRECIATE
THE PROMPT RETURN OF THIS BOOK.]   77

A CHARGE IS MADE FOR OVERDUE MATERIALS

WITHDRAWN